I fainted when I saw this yogi
magician, Delhi, about 1340.

Native boats, filled with fresh fruit and fish, coming to greet us, Sumatra, 1346.

I walked around the Rock of Gibraltar, 1350.

I climbed this tower, called a
minaret, and got a fine view,
Marrakesh, 1351.

Gathering rainwater from a natural well inside the trunk of a baobab tree, Sahara, 1352.

Hippos—the first I had ever seen—feeding on the shore
in the moonlight, Black Nile, 1353.

For my mother

Arabic and Chinese calligraphy and illuminated maps and pages are by the author.
Arabic spellings of place names reflect fourteenth-century orthography.

www.houghtonmifflinbooks.com

The text of this book is set in Adobe Caslon.

Library of Congress Cataloging-in-Publication Data

Rumford, James.
Traveling man : the journey of Ibn Battuta, 1325–1354 /
written and illustrated by James Rumford.
p.   cm.
ISBN 0-618-08366-9
1. Ibn Batutta, 1304–1377 — Journeys — Juvenile literature. 2. Voyages and travels —
Juvenile literature. 3. Asia — Description and travel — Juvenile literature.
4. Africa — Description and travel — Juvenile literature. 5. Travelers — Islamic
Empire — Biography — Juvenile literature. [1. Ibn Battuta, 1304–1377.
2. Travelers. 3. Voyages and travels.] I. Title.
G370.I2 R86 2001
910'.92 — dc21
00-057257

Printed in Singapore
TWP 10 9 8 7 6 5 4 3 2 1

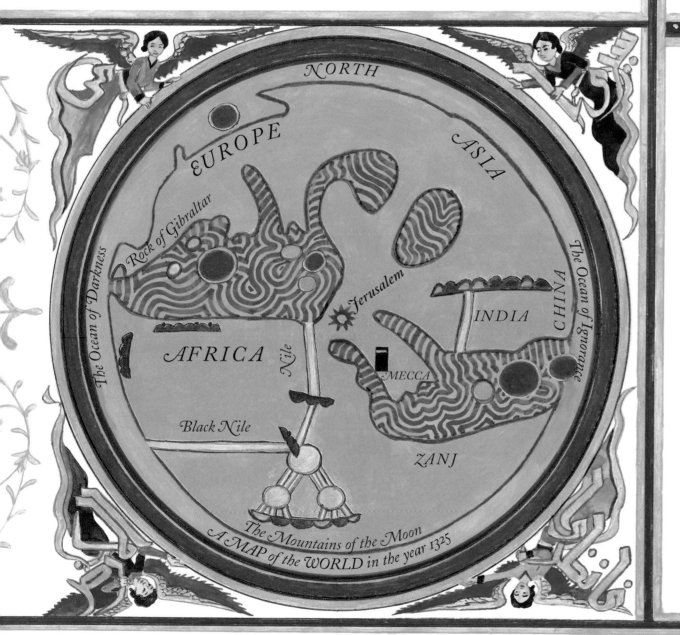

Traveling Man

*The Journey of
Ibn Battuta, 1325–1354*

Written, illustrated, and illuminated by

James Rumford

HOUGHTON MIFFLIN COMPANY

BOSTON · 2001

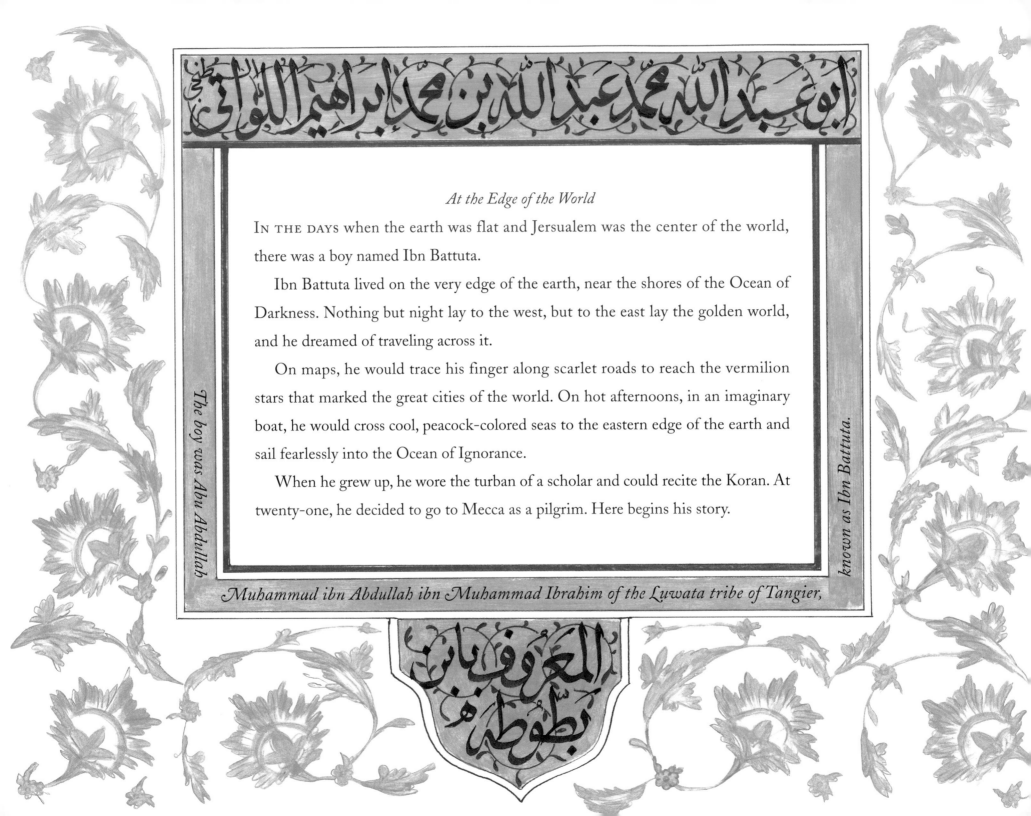

ابو عبد الله محمد عبد الله بن محمد ابراهيم اللواتي

At the Edge of the World

IN THE DAYS when the earth was flat and Jersualem was the center of the world, there was a boy named Ibn Battuta.

Ibn Battuta lived on the very edge of the earth, near the shores of the Ocean of Darkness. Nothing but night lay to the west, but to the east lay the golden world, and he dreamed of traveling across it.

On maps, he would trace his finger along scarlet roads to reach the vermilion stars that marked the great cities of the world. On hot afternoons, in an imaginary boat, he would cross cool, peacock-colored seas to the eastern edge of the earth and sail fearlessly into the Ocean of Ignorance.

When he grew up, he wore the turban of a scholar and could recite the Koran. At twenty-one, he decided to go to Mecca as a pilgrim. Here begins his story.

The boy was Abu Abdullah

known as Ibn Battuta.

Muhammad ibn Abdullah ibn Muhammad Ibrahim of the Luwata tribe of Tangier,

المعروف بابن بطوطه

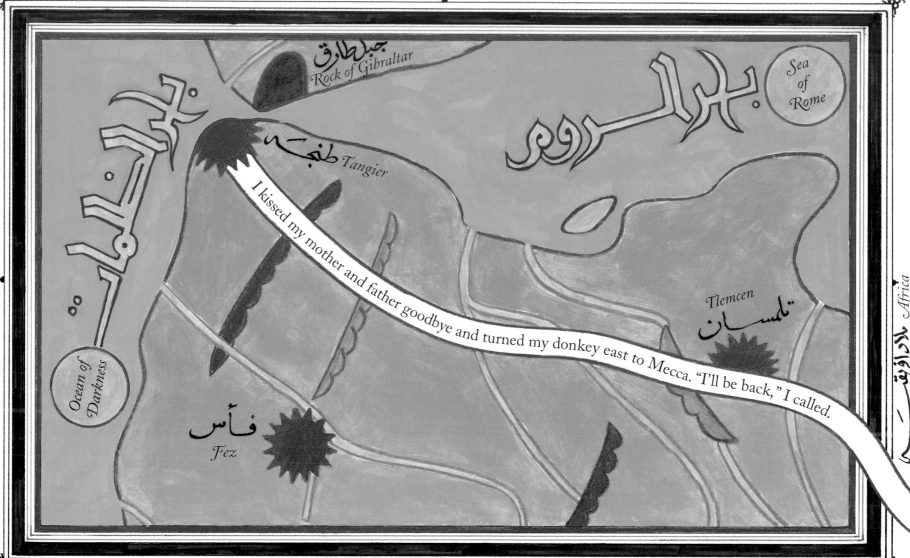

I kissed my mother and father goodbye and turned my donkey east to Mecca. "I'll be back," I called.

Rock of Gibraltar

Sea of Rome

Tangier

Tlemcen

Ocean of Darkness

Fez

Africa

The Land of the Blacks

A Map of Morocco, 1325

كان خروجي من طنجة مسقط رأسي في يوم الخميس الثاني

من شهر الله... عام خمسة وعشرين وسبعمائة

I joined a group of merchants and they told me of the marvels that lay ahead.

معتمداً حج منفرداً عن رفيق...

The Lonely Road

BANDITS ROAMED the countryside like wolves. They stalked stragglers and hunted down lonely pilgrims. I tried to keep up. I even got rid of my extra baggage.

Then I fell ill. Too weak to hold on, I unwound my turban and tied myself in the saddle.

At last, after hours of riding, we reached the gates of a large city and safety. People ran out to greet us. Friends found friends, but there was no one to greet me. Tears of loneliness filled my eyes.

Then a man turned to me and smiled, saying, "Welcome, pilgrim. Welcome to our home."

"Traveling," I said to myself later. "It makes you lonely, then gives you a friend."

They also told me of the dangers.

Tunis

Tripoli

This odd meeting place of caravans — it's called the world! —OMAR KHAYYĀM

I was well again. I joined a caravan, and with the *jang-jarang* of camel bells, we were off!

Sirt

سرت

As I entered Egypt, I saw the wealth that the River Nile had brought to the people—gold, incense, and abundant food.

برقة

Al-Marj

Alexandria

الإسكندرية

مصر

Cairo

A Night in the Land Watered by the Moon

THE EGYPTIANS were as generous as the Nile. Because I was a scholar and a pilgrim, they gave me alms: food, money, and a place to sleep.

Near Alexandria, a holy man invited me to stay in his house and sleep on his roof. That night, a giant bird snatched me up and carried me on its back far beyond Mecca. Then I woke up.

"Not only will you go to Mecca," said the holy man when I told him my dream, "but you will also travel to the edge of the earth. When you get to India, my brother Dilshad will save your life."

Then, before I could say a word, the holy man hurried me on my way.

بحر النيل

Nile River

نيل السودان

Black Nile

جبل القمر

Mountains of the Moon

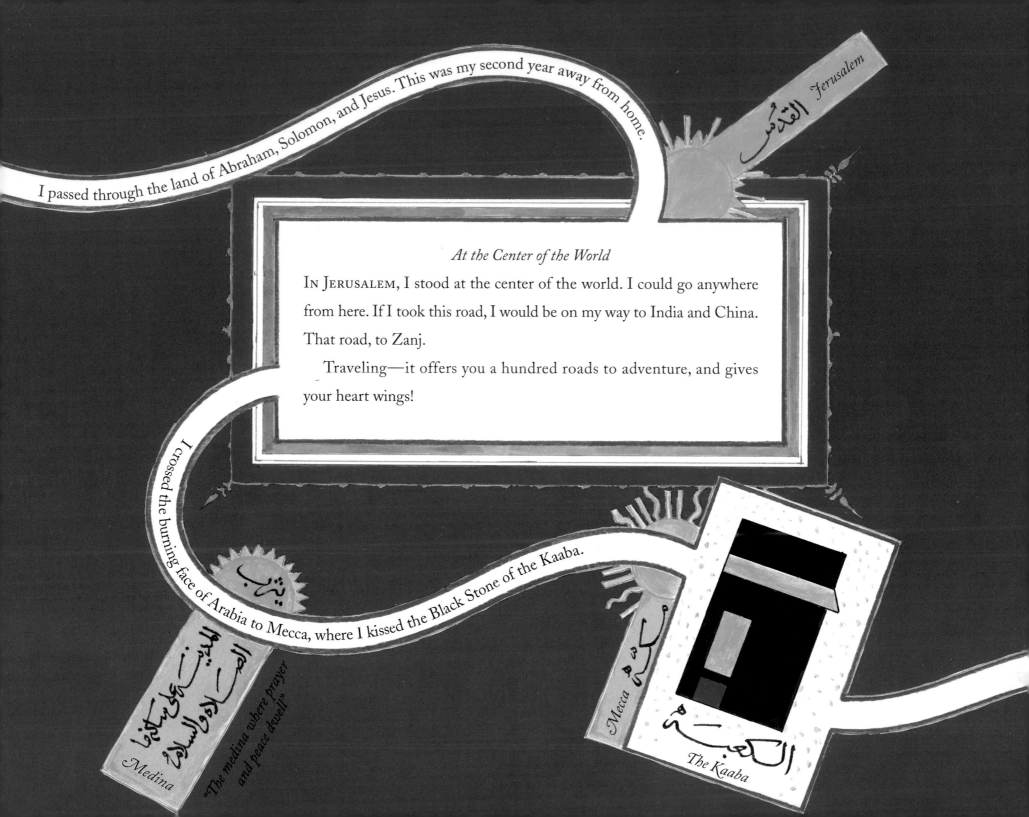

I passed through the land of Abraham, Solomon, and Jesus. This was my second year away from home.

Jerusalem
القدس

At the Center of the World

IN JERUSALEM, I stood at the center of the world. I could go anywhere from here. If I took this road, I would be on my way to India and China. That road, to Zanj.

Traveling—it offers you a hundred roads to adventure, and gives your heart wings!

I crossed the burning face of Arabia to Mecca, where I kissed the Black Stone of the Kaaba.

Medina
يثرب
المدينة على ساكنها الصلاة والسلام
"The medina where prayer and peace dwell"

Mecca
مكة

The Kaaba
الكعبة

IBN BATTUTA IN JERUSALEM

I traveled to Iraq and met rich sultans. I crossed into Persia and saw golden mosques.

Baghdad

Isfahan

In my fifth year from home, I took a boat.

South to Zanj

HOT, SALTY WAVES crashed onto the ship. At first, I was terrified, but slowly I learned to love the sea. We sailed down the coast of ivory and ebony, of gold dust and leopard skins. I could find no words to describe the beauty I saw.

Everywhere I went, sultans asked me about my home and about my travels. Under warm African stars, I found the words I needed and told them all I could.

Traveling—it leaves you speechless, then turns you into a storyteller.

Kilwa

I made some friends and we daydreamed of going to India and becoming rich.

Bukhara بخارا

Samarkand سمرقند

Balkh بلخ

Kabul کابل

ا د را ک

We crossed the steppes of Asia. We trudged through the cold Hindu-Killing Mountains, warming our thoughts on the promise of Indian gold.

آب بنج

We crossed the Five Waters. We did not see the rhinos hiding in tall reeds or the rebels lying in wait. Suddenly I was hit by an arrow.

مُلتان
Multan

The Five Waters

Even though I was wounded, I helped my companions fight off the rebels, and we continued on to Delhi.

By the time we reached the sultan's palace, my wound had healed.

Delhi

To the Land of Flying Money

THE SULTAN'S PALACE in Delhi was huge. In one great hall were elephants bowing to the sultan and catapults flinging gold coins out to the people. Into this hall I entered. Because I was a scholar, the sultan made me Judge of Delhi. After nine years of traveling, I was a rich man.

If I pleased the sultan, money. If I displeased him, death. Once, I so angered him that he sent assassins after me. But I had a plan. They would not kill me while I prayed, so for nine days I prayed, until they finally left. What kind of life was this? I gave everything away and sought happiness as a poor man.

The sultan wanted me back, but he had nothing I wanted. Then he offered to send me to China as his ambassador. He knew my heart. I could not refuse. I was on the road again and rich—but for how long?

Jewels poured forth; the attendants scattered coins, like a rain of blossoms on the meadow. —JĀMĪ

We left in a great procession.

We crossed into rebel territory.

The One Road

THE REBELS ATTACKED, and I was captured. They planned to kill me, but I outwitted them. I told them I was nobody—just a traveling man. I talked and talked until I talked them into letting me go. I began walking. Days passed. Without food, I grew weak. Then a man appeared.

"I am Dilshad," he said. "Follow me."

"I can't walk."

"Then climb up on my shoulders, and I will carry you."

I fainted. When I awoke, I was among my companions again and Dilshad was gone. Then I remembered the words of the holy man in Egypt.

Traveling—it offers you a hundred roads. How does a holy man know the one you'll take?

I found a lotus tree and hungrily grabbed at the ripened fruit, tearing my hands on the thorns.

My companions rejoiced to see me alive. We continued on our way.

We passed through the land of man-eating tigers, arriving at the coast of monsoons and ship-eating seas.

We entered the great port of Calicut.

Calicut تفالسقوت

On the Shores of Good Fortune

CHINESE JUNKS as big as palaces awaited us, their captains anxious to leave before the sky broke open. Some ships left the first day we arrived. Others stayed, huddled in the harbor.

Then the storm came. It spread its black wings over the sea and sank the Chinese ships.

Everything was lost. I alone was spared, for I had stayed ashore for Friday prayers. I knelt on the beach and gave thanks for my life.

I could not go back to Delhi with bad news. The sultan would kill me.

So, in my eighteenth year from home, I boarded a boat.

Past Paradise

IN THE MALDIVES, a vizier made me a judge and gave me a chest of jewels. I was rich but restless. Beyond the horizon was China and the edge of the world, so I left in a boat.

The boat took me past a tiny island struggling to stay dry above the waves. A man lived there with his family in a small house shaded by coconut trees. Here was paradise! Suddenly, I wanted so much to be that man and have a home.

سَرَنْديب
Serendib

جاوه
Jawa

I waved, but the boat carried me away like a soaring bird.

I sailed to China on a glasslike sea. This was my twentieth year from home.

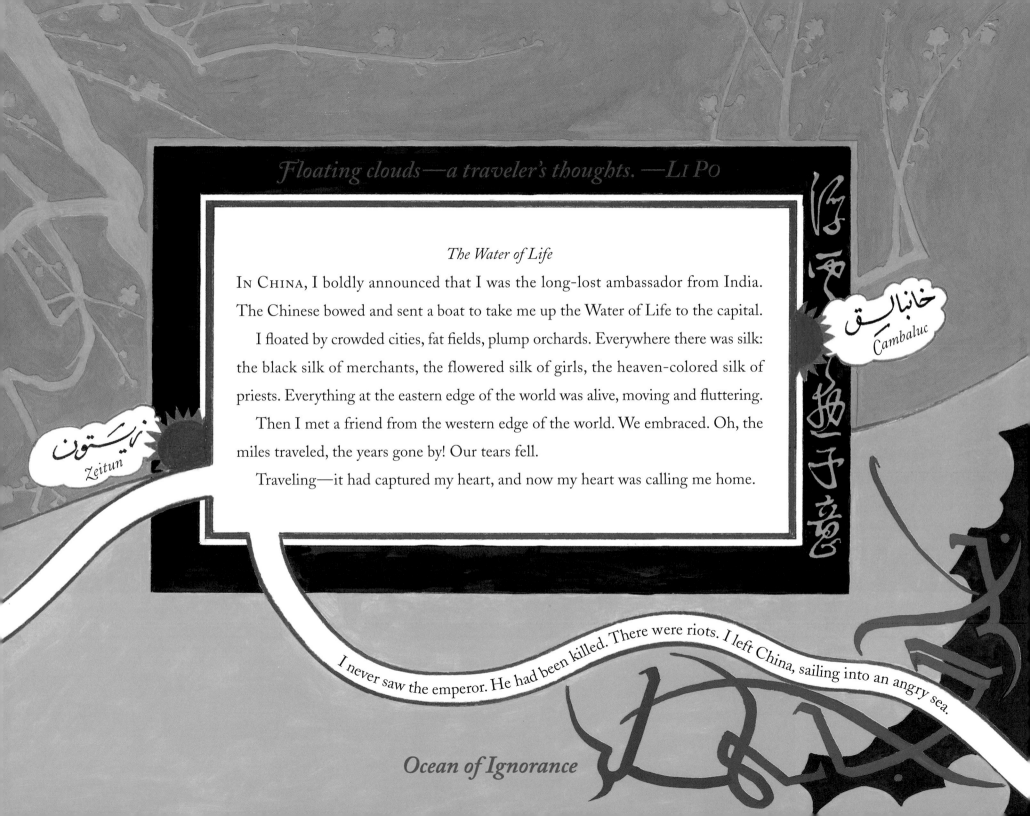

Floating clouds—a traveler's thoughts. —LI PO

خانبالـق
Cambaluc

 زيـتون
Zeitun

The Water of Life

IN CHINA, I boldly announced that I was the long-lost ambassador from India. The Chinese bowed and sent a boat to take me up the Water of Life to the capital.

I floated by crowded cities, fat fields, plump orchards. Everywhere there was silk: the black silk of merchants, the flowered silk of girls, the heaven-colored silk of priests. Everything at the eastern edge of the world was alive, moving and fluttering.

Then I met a friend from the western edge of the world. We embraced. Oh, the miles traveled, the years gone by! Our tears fell.

Traveling—it had captured my heart, and now my heart was calling me home.

I never saw the emperor. He had been killed. There were riots. I left China, sailing into an angry sea.

Ocean of Ignorance

Lost, we headed blindly into the Ocean of Ignorance toward earth's last horizon, going farther than I had dared travel in my boyhood dreams.

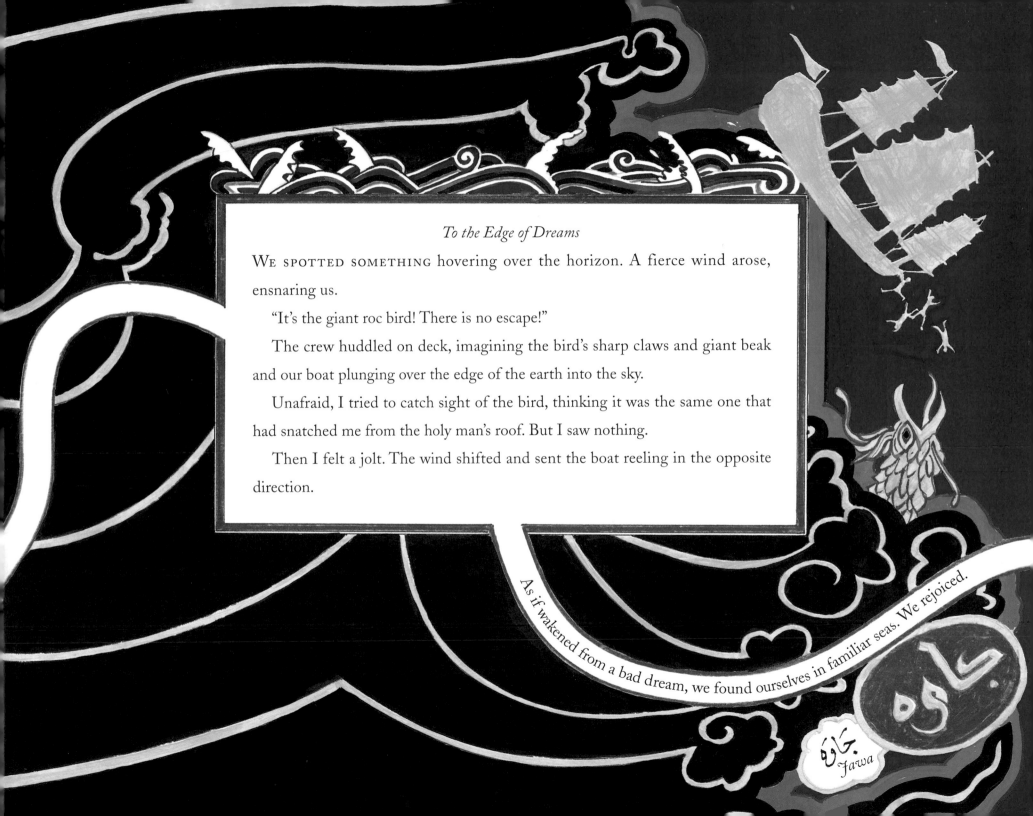

To the Edge of Dreams

WE SPOTTED SOMETHING hovering over the horizon. A fierce wind arose, ensnaring us.

"It's the giant roc bird! There is no escape!"

The crew huddled on deck, imagining the bird's sharp claws and giant beak and our boat plunging over the edge of the earth into the sky.

Unafraid, I tried to catch sight of the bird, thinking it was the same one that had snatched me from the holy man's roof. But I saw nothing.

Then I felt a jolt. The wind shifted and sent the boat reeling in the opposite direction.

As if wakened from a bad dream, we found ourselves in familiar seas. We rejoiced.

In my twenty-second year from home I made my way back to Jerusalem.

Jerusalem

Death Black As Night

AT THE CENTER of the world, the plague lay in wait. Everywhere there was death. Everywhere there were peopleless cities.

In Damascus, I learned that my father had died fifteen years earlier. When I was only a few miles from home, I heard that my mother had just died from the plague. I wept.

In my hometown, a boy asked me if I was lost. I only smiled.

Traveling—it gives you a home in a thousand strange places, then leaves you a stranger in your own land.

Tangier

I left, a wanderer. I walked around the Rock of Gibraltar.

Timbuktu

I crossed the Sahara and rested under giant baobab trees. Near the Black Nile, I was almost eaten by a crocodile!

In my twenty-ninth year of traveling, I received a letter from the sultan of Morocco, offering me a place to live for as long as I wished.

طنجة
Tangier

شمس الدين رحمه الله

A Traveler's Reward

IBN BATTUTA RETURNED not with the wealth of jewels or gold coins but with the wealth of a traveler—his memories.

In an age of few books, he spun these memories into stories and led his listeners down scarlet roads and opened their eyes to the world. In boats made of words, he took his friends across peacock-colored seas and showed them new horizons.

"I wish I could go where you went, see what you saw," a child once said.

"You can," said the old traveler, his eyes aglow. "Traveling—all you do is take the first step."

تحفة النظار في غرائب الأمصار وعجائب الاسفار

I kissed the letter and headed home.

فاس
Fez

IBN BATTUTA *(ih-ben bah-too-ta)* was born in Tangier *(tan-jeer)*, Morocco, in 1304 and died in Morocco probably in 1369. In 1355, after almost thirty years of traveling and 75,000 miles, he told his story to the Moroccan court secretary IBN JUZAYY *(ih-ben jooz-eye)*, who wrote it down in Arabic. You can still see Ibn Juzayy's original handwritten book at the National Library in Paris.

The story you have read is an adaptation of what Ibn Juzayy wrote. There is a longer English version by H. GIBB called *Travels in Asia and Africa 1325–1354*. In it you will read about Ibn Battuta's many other adventures, learn more about the places he visited, and meet this deeply religious man who was called "the traveler of his age."

Below is more information about some of the people, places, and things mentioned in the story.

Africa once meant modern Tunisia, not the entire continent.

Alms in this story are money, food, or lodging given to a pilgrim.

The **baobab** *(bay-oh-bob)* is an African tree with a giant trunk.

The **Black Nile** is the Niger *(nigh-juhr)* River.

The **Black Stone** is a sacred stone built into the wall of the Kaaba.

Calicut *(cal-e-cut)* is an Indian port. Its name gave us the word *calico*.

Cambaluc *(kahm-ball-uck)* or Khanbaliq *(hahn-ball-ick)* was the Mongolian name for Beijing *(bay-jing)*.

A **caravan** is a group of travelers journeying together.

The **Five Waters** are the five main rivers in the Punjab *(poon-jahb)*, which literally means "five waters." These rivers flow into the Indus.

Friday is the holy day of the week for Muslims.

Hindu-Killing Mountains is a literal translation of *Hindu Kush*.

Jāmī (1414–1492) was a Persian poet born in what is now Afghanistan.

Jawa is Java and maybe parts of Malaysia and Sumatra.

Jerusalem was put at the center of the world by some Arab mapmakers.

A **judge** or *qādī (cah-dee)* knows the religious laws of Muslims, settles disputes, and brings harmony to the community.

A **junk** is a boat with rectangular sails stiffened with bamboo.

The **Kaaba** *(cah-ah-bah)* is a small building in Mecca which holds a black stone. The Kaaba is a sacred place for Muslims.

The **Koran** or Qur'ān *(core-on)* is the holy book of the Muslims.

The **Land of the Blacks** meant most of modern Africa. The Arabic word for Blacks is *Sūdān*, now the name of an African country.

Li Po or Li Bo (701–762) was a Tang Dynasty Chinese poet.

The **lotus tree** is a kind of jujube *(joo-joob)*.

The **Luwata tribe** was a Berber tribe of North Africa.

Mecca *(meck-kah)* is a holy city in Saudi Arabia for Muslims.

A **medina** is the Arabic word for city.

A **minaret** *(min-are-ret)* is a tower on a mosque.

The **monsoons** (from the Arabic *mawsim*, "season") are great rains.

Morocco (or *Al-Maghrib* in Arabic) means "The West," because it was once the western edge of the known world.

A **mosque** *(mosk)* is a Muslim house of worship.

The **Mountains of the Moon** are the Ruhenzoris of Rwanda and were once believed to be the source of the River Nile.

Ocean of Darkness is an old Arab name for the Atlantic Ocean.

Ocean of Ignorance is a rare Arab name for the Pacific Ocean. This name might also be translated as the *Uncharted Ocean*.

Omar Khayyām (1048–1122) was a Persian poet and mathematician.

Persia is an old name for Iran.

A **pilgrim** in this story is a Muslim who goes to Mecca. All Muslims should go to Mecca at least once.

The **plague** *(playg)* is the bubonic plague or Black Death, which killed millions. Ibn Battuta says that in Cairo, 20,000 people died a day.

A **roc** *(rock)* is a giant mythical bird.

The **Sea of Rome**, or The Sea of Byzantium *(biz-an-chee-um)*, was the Arab name for the Mediterranean Sea.

Serendib *(sair-en-deeb)* is Sri Lanka. The name is the source of the word *serendipity*, which means discovering something fortunate by accident.

The **steppes** *(steps)* are the grassy plains of central Asia.

A **sultan** is a ruler or king.

A **vizier** *(vih-zeer)* is an official who gives advice to the ruler.

The **Water of Life** may refer to China's Grand Canal, a series of canals that connects Hangzhou *(hahng-joe)* with Beijing.

A **yogi** *(yo-ghee)* is a Hindu who can do amazing things because he has learned to control both his body and his mind.

Zanj *(zahnj)* is Zanzibar and East Africa.

Zeitun *(zay-toon)* is the Chinese port of Quanzhou *(chwahn-joe)*. Zaytun probably gave us the word for *satin*.

A Map of the Travels of Ibn Battuta, 1325–1354

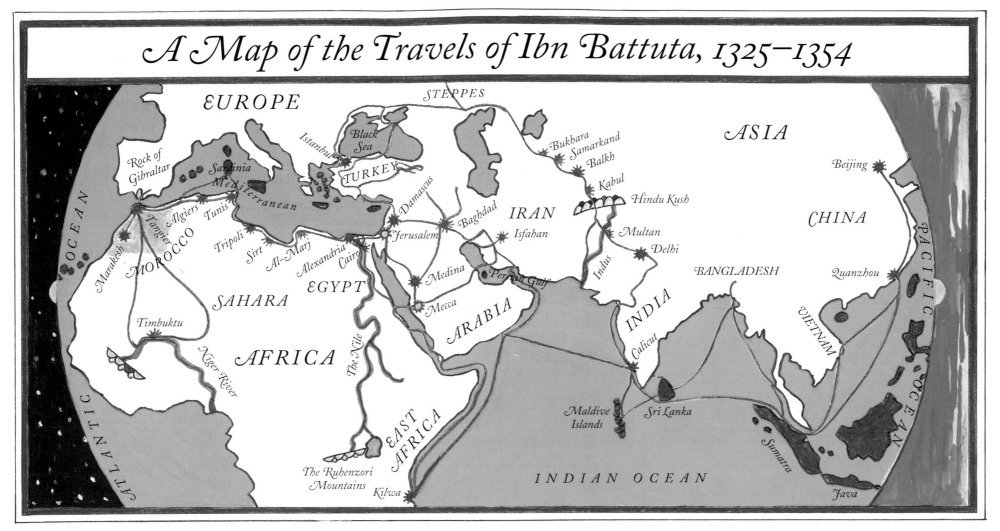

Translations by the author of the Arabic, Persian, and Chinese phrases along the margins of the story can be located by referring to the pictures indicated below:

[Ibn Battuta and the merchants] "I left my birthplace of Tangier on Thursday, June 14, 1325, to go on a pilgrimage . . . alone, without friends. . . ." —Ibn Battuta

[Ibn Battuta in Jerusalem] "I entered [the Holy Man's room] one day and he said to me, 'So, you love to travel and roam about from country to country, do you?' I said to him, 'Yes, I do.'" —Ibn Battuta

[Rebels and the tiger] "And [Dilshad] said to me, 'Say: God is enough for us and an excellent counselor.'" —Ibn Battuta

[Chinese junk] "Indigo-colored clouds came up from an indigo sea." —Farrūkhī (far-roo-hee), Persian, d. 1038

[The angels, left side] "On the other side of the mountain I was cut off from news of home. Now that winter is over and spring is here, I head home. I feel uneasy, too afraid to ask news from passersby." —Li Pin (lee pin), Tang Dynasty

[The angels, right side] "Young I left; old I return. The village sounds haven't changed but my hair is now so thin. The children and I see each other, but they don't know me. Laughing, they ask where the traveler is from." —He Zhizhang (huh juhr-jahng), 659–744

[A traveler's reward, top] Shams-ud-Din (shahms-ood-dean) [another name for Ibn Battuta followed by the Muslim equivalent of "rest in peace"]

[A traveler's reward, bottom] [The title of Ibn Battuta's book] A Presentation by an Observer, on the Wonders of Great Cities and the Marvels of the Road

The Pyramids, Egypt, 1326.

North of the Black Sea, 1333. Trying to keep warm by wearing all my clothes.

Dressed in pilgrim's clothes, 1326.

With my beautiful black horse, India, 1336.

Constantinople (Istanbul), 1332. With the Christian emperor's father, who touched my hands and feet because I had been to Jerusalem.